Draw Your Own Encyclopaedia

Our Solar System
Classroom Edition

Colin M. Drysdale

Pictish Beast Publications

Text Copyright © 2018, 2019 Colin M. Drysdale
Imprint and Layout Copyright © 2019 Colin M. Drysdale/Pictish Beast Publications

All rights reserved.
This is the classroom edition of *Draw Your Own Encyclopaedia Our Solar System*. This means that the cost of this book includes the right to photocopy its contents to produce handouts for use in classrooms and for other educational purposes. However, they cannot be reproduced for any 'for-profit' activity without express permission.

ISBN - 978-1-909832-66-4
Published by Pictish Beast Publications, Glasgow, UK.
Published in the United Kingdom
First Printing: 2019. First Edition.

A non-classroom edition of this book for individual children is also available (ISBN: 978-1-909832-46-6).

The cover image is copyright © Alhovik/Shutterstock.com

www.PictishBeastPublications.com

Introduction

This book is part of the *Draw Your Own Encyclopaedia* series of factual books for children aged six to twelve. It provides interesting introductions to a variety of different features of our solar system. This classroom edition is aimed at teachers and other educators (rather than at individual children, as is the case for the individual edition). It contains:

- Eleven double-page spreads which explore a range of topics about our solar system that can be photocopied to create handouts for use in the classroom or as homework assignments. Each one contains an introductory question, a paragraph that explores its topic, questions to test your students comprehension of the contents of this paragraph, quick facts to provide additional information, and space for the student to add their own illustration for this topic.

- A blank *Draw Your Own Encyclopaedia* double-page spread which you can photocopy and hand out to your students to allow them to create their own custom encyclopaedia entry based on a topic related to our solar system of their (or your) choice.

- Two handouts which you can use to introduce mathematics into your lessons about our solar system. The first allows your students to calculate the weight of a two-pint bottle of milk on different planets, while the second allows them to calculate their age based on the length of a year on each planet.

- A sixteen-question pop quiz that you can use to test your students knowledge about our solar system. All the information needed to answer these questions is contained in the eleven double-page spreads from this book.

- Links to additional background information about the solar system which you can use to increase your own knowledge of this subject.

- Links to free online content, such as videos, related to the topics covered in this book that you can show to your students.

- Ideas for four interactive and fun additional classroom activities.

- Data sheets detailing and comparing key characteristics of the different planets, and selected other objects, in our solar system. The information on these data sheets can be used to support a range of additional classroom activities.

Thus, taken together, the contents of this book provide you with all the information you need to teach your class all about our solar system in a fun and interesting way that integrates factual knowledge, reading comprehension, maths skills and practical demonstrations.

What Is A Solar System?

A solar system consists of a star and all the objects in space that orbit around it. Our solar system formed around 4.6 billion years ago from a cloud of interstellar dust left over from the explosion of an older, and much larger, star. Today, our solar system consists of our sun, 8 planets, at least 525 moons, and many hundreds of thousands of minor planets, asteroids and comets. Based on the furthest observable object (a minor planet called Sedna), it is about 287 billion kilometres in diameter. Sedna is so far from the Sun, it takes the Sun's light about five and a half days to reach it!

Questions To Answer:

1. What is a solar system?

2. How old is our solar system?

3. How many planets are there in our solar system?

4. What is the diameter of the solar system?

5. What is the name of the furthest observable object?

Quick Fact: The sun is actually a star. While it has no official scientific name, it is sometimes referred to by the Latin name Sol.

Quick Fact: The nearest neighbouring solar system is called Proxima Centauri. It is approximately 40 trillion kilometres away!

Draw a picture of our solar system showing the sun at the centre and the relative positions of the eight planets that orbit around it. Write down the name of each planet beside its image.

What Is The Largest Planet In Our Solar System?

The largest planet in our solar system is Jupiter. It is 139,822 kilometres in diameter and weighs the same as 318 planet Earths. This means that while it is a thousand times lighter than the sun, its mass is two and a half times the mass of all the other planets in the solar system combined. Jupiter is what is known as a gas giant. This means it does not have a solid surface and it is mainly made from a mixture of gases and liquids. Jupiter is about 778 million kilometres away from the sun, and it takes almost twelve Earth years to complete a single orbit of the sun.

Questions To Answer:

1. What is the largest planet in our solar system?

2. What is its diameter?

3. How many planet Earths does it weigh?

4. How far away from the Sun is this planet?

5. How long does it take this planet to orbit the Sun?

Quick Fact: The smallest planet in our solar system is Mercury. It is 4,879 kilometres in diameter. This means that it is one-third the size of the Earth.

Draw pictures of the largest and the smallest planets in our solar system, side by side, using the same scale for each one so you can see how different they are in size.

Quick Fact: Jupiter is famous for its Great Red Spot. This is a storm that has been raging in its atmosphere for at least 188 years, and possibly much, much longer. It is 16,350 kilometres in diameter, making this single storm larger than the whole of planet Earth!

Is Pluto A Planet?

Until very recently, Pluto was considered to be the ninth planet in our solar system. However, in 2006, the International Astronomical Union downgraded it to a dwarf planet. For an object to be considered a full planet, it must fulfil three criteria: 1. It must orbit the sun; 2. It must have a sufficient mass so that gravity makes it form a more-or-less round shape; 3. It has to have cleared its orbit of other objects. While Pluto orbits the sun and is more-or-less round, there are other objects which share its orbit. This means it isn't big enough to have cleared these objects away.

Questions To Answer:

1. When was Pluto downgraded to a dwarf planet?

2. What are the three things a space object has to do to be considered a planet?

   A.

   B.

   C.

Quick Fact: Pluto is one of five dwarf planets that have so far been given names. The others are Ceres, Haumea, Makemake and Eris. However, there may be several hundred more out there that have yet to be given official names.

Draw a picture of Pluto here, and under it, write its name. See if you can find out how big it is, and write its diameter down alongside its name.

Quick Fact: Pluto was only discovered in 1930 by Clyde Tombaugh of the Lowell Observatory in Flagstaff, Arizona, USA. It was named after the ancient Greek god of the underworld. The name was first suggested by Venetia Burney who, at the time, was eleven years old.

How Hot Is The Sun?

The sun is almost 1.4 million kilometres in diameter, and it is effectively a very large ball of burning gas. It is primarily made of hydrogen, and its heat and light are generated by the fusion of hydrogen nuclei to form helium. The surface of the sun is around 5,500 degrees centigrade. That makes it ten times hotter than the coals of a barbecue. The light from the sun travels at 299,792 kilometres per second, and despite the 150 million kilometres that separate the Sun from the Earth, it only takes eight minutes for its light to reach us.

Quick Fact: The surface is not the hottest part of the sun. In solar flares, which are eruptions of hot gas, temperatures can reach up to 100 million degrees!

Quick Fact: One of the coldest places in the solar system is the south-western edge of Hermite Crater on the Moon. Here, temperatures can be as low as -247 °C.

Questions To Answer:

1. How hot is the surface of the Sun?

2. What is the hottest part of the Sun?

3. How cold is it in Hermite Crater on the moon?

From *Draw Your Own Encyclopaedia Our Solar System* by Colin M. Drysdale

As well as generating heat and light, the sun also generates a solar wind. These are charged particles that stream out from it. When they hit the Earth's magnetic fields, they create the northern and southern lights. Draw a picture here to show what the northern lights look like.

Quick Fact: It takes the light from the sun only three minutes to reach Mercury (the closest planet) and just over four hours to reach Neptune (the furthest planet). However, it takes the sun's light four years to reach Alpha Centauri, our closest neighbouring star!

Which Planet Has The Longest Day?

A day is defined as the length of time it takes a planet to complete one full spin on its axis. On Earth, this takes just under twenty-four hours. However, on different planets, days have different lengths. At just under ten hours, Jupiter has the shortest days, while on Venus (which has the longest days) each day lasts 5,832 hours (or 243 Earth days!). A year (the time it takes a planet to complete a single orbit around the sun) also varies between planets. Mercury takes only 88 Earth days to orbit the sun, while the Earth takes 365 days. In contrast, it takes almost 165 Earth years for Neptune to complete one orbit!

Questions To Answer:

1. What is the definition of a day?

2. How long is a day on Jupiter?

3. Which planet has the longest day?

From *Draw Your Own Encyclopaedia Our Solar System* by Colin M. Drysdale

Venus takes 243 Earth days to rotate once on its axis, but it only takes just under 225 Earth days to orbit the Sun. This means that on Venus, a day is longer than a year! Draw a picture of Venus here, and write its day length and year length underneath it.

Quick Fact: Venus is unusual in another way, too. While almost all planets in our solar system rotate clockwise, it rotates in the opposite direction. This means that unlike on Earth, on Venus, the Sun rises in the west and sets in the east!

What Is An Asteroid?

Asteroids are pieces of rock that orbit the Sun, but which are too small to be considered planets. Asteroids must have a diameter of at least one metre, and can be as large as tens or hundreds of kilometres across. They are only found in the inner solar system, and most of them are found in the Asteroid Belt between Mars and Jupiter. Rocky asteroid-like objects are also found in the outer solar system, especially in the Kuiper Belt (which is beyond the orbit of Neptune) and in the Oort Cloud at the very edge of our solar system. However, despite their similarities, these are no longer classified as asteroids.

Quick Fact: The many craters that can be seen on the surface of the moon were created by asteroids hitting it.

Quick Fact: An asteroid hitting the Earth is thought to have been one of the main factors that caused the extinction of the dinosaurs!

Questions To Answer:

1. What is an asteroid?

2. Where are most asteroids found?

3. How big are asteroids?

From *Draw Your Own Encyclopaedia Our Solar System* by Colin M. Drysdale

The asteroid that caused the extinction of the dinosaurs is thought to have been between ten and fifteen kilometres in diameter. Draw a picture of what you think this impact would have looked like when it happened.

Where Do Comets Come From?

Unlike asteroids, which are made of rock, comets are mostly made of ice. Most comets in our solar system come from the Oort Cloud, a vast ring containing millions of objects at the very edge of our solar system. Many of these objects are thought to have been formed at the very birth of our solar system. Occasionally, the orbit of one of these objects is disturbed, sending it shooting towards the sun. As it enters the inner solar system, the heat from the sun starts to melt it, creating a long tail of debris and making it much more easily visible.

Quick Fact: One of the most famous comets in the solar system is Halley's comet. It was discovered in 1705 by Edmund Halley. It is a short-period comet, meaning that it takes less than 200 Earth years to orbit the sun. Halley's comet was last seen from Earth in 1986, and it is expected to return again in the 2060s.

Questions To Answer:

1. What are comets made from?

2. Where do most comets come from?

3. When will Halley's comet next be seen from Earth?

Halley's comet visits the inner solar system approximately once every seventy-six years. In the past, it was often seen as a predictor that something either very good or very bad was about to happen. Draw a picture of Halley's comet, with its long tail, as it appeared last time it visited the inner solar system in 1986.

Quick Fact: Much of the water on Earth is thought to have come from icy comets that collided with it when it was very young.

Quick Fact: No matter the direction it is moving in, a comet's tail always points away from the Sun.

How Long Would It Take To Get To Mars?

Earth and Mars are neighbouring planets in the solar system, but working out how long it would take to get from Earth to Mars is not as easy as it may seem. This is because both the Earth and Mars orbit the Sun. When the Earth and Mars are both on the same side of the Sun, they are under 60 million kilometres apart. When they are on opposite sides, they are up to 401 million kilometres away from each other. In theory, our fastest space craft could get to Mars in as little as 40 days, but its launch would need to be timed perfectly. In practice, however, it would probably take between 150 and 250 days.

Questions To Answer:

1. How close are Mars and Earth at their closest?

2. What is the furthest distance apart that they are?

3. How long would it take to get from Earth to Mars?

While no humans have visited Mars so far, we have sent a wide range of unmanned space craft there. These include the ones that carried the Mars Rovers. These were semi-autonomous vehicles that we used to help us learn more about Mars. Draw a picture here of one of these Rovers surveying the surface of Mars.

Quick Fact: Mars is known as the red planet because it is covered in a layer of red dust. This red dust is mostly made of iron, and it's red because it has become oxidised by exposure to the thin Martian atmosphere. Here on Earth, we call this type of red dust rust, so Mars is not only the red planet, it is also the rusty planet!

Is There Life On Other Planets In Our Solar System?

Since Earth is teeming with life, it's only reasonable to wonder if there's also life elsewhere in our solar system. Scientists have spent many years looking for life on other planets, but so far, they have yet to find any definitive evidence of life anywhere other than on Earth. However, this does not mean that there isn't life elsewhere. It might just mean it hasn't been found yet. The most likely places in our solar system, other than Earth, where there might be life are Mars, some of the moons of Jupiter and Saturn, and Pluto. These places all either have, or had, liquid environments which could host microbial life.

Can you name three places in the solar system, other than Earth, where life could potentially exist?

A.

B.

C.

If life does exist elsewhere in our solar system, what do you think it would look like? Would it look the same as life on Earth, or would it look very different because of very different conditions on other planets? Draw a picture of what you think alien life might look like here.

Quick Fact: For the first billion years of life on Earth, the only living things were microorganisms.

Quick Fact: If Earth is the only place in the solar system where life exists, then it makes it all the more important to protect it!

Do Other Planets Have Moons?

A moon is an object which directly orbits another object in space other than the Sun. Most people are familiar with the Earth's moon (also known as Luna, its Latin name), but it is only one of 525 known moons in our solar system. The only planets that don't have any moons are the two that are closest to the Sun (Mercury and Venus), while Mars has two moons. In contrast, Saturn has at least sixty-two moons, while Jupiter has at least sixty-nine. This includes Europa and Callisto, which are both places where life could potentially exist beyond Earth.

Quick Fact: Of the 525 known moons in the solar system, only 178 orbit planets. The rest orbit minor planetary bodies, including the dwarf planets of Pluto (which has five moons), Haumes (2), Makemake (1) and Eris (1).

Questions To Answer:

1. What is a moon?

2. How many moons are their in our solar system?

3. Which planet has the most moons?

While our Moon seems very big to us, it is not the largest moon in our Solar System. Instead, the largest moon is called Ganymede and it orbits Jupiter. Ganymede has a diameter of over 5,000 kilometres, making it twice as big as our moon, and larger than the planet Mercury! Draw a picture of Ganymede here.

Quick Fact: The moon is the only place in our Solar System, other than Earth, that humans have visited. Between 1969 and 1972, the moon was visited on six occasions, and only twelve people have ever set foot on it. The longest time anyone has ever stayed on the moon was just over three days.

What Will Happen When The Sun Runs Out Of Fuel?

The main fuel that keeps the sun burning is hydrogen, and it burns around 600 million tons of it per second. However, there is enough hydrogen left in the Sun to keep it going for another five billion years. Once all its fuel has been used up, the Sun will turn into a type of star known as a red giant. As it does this, its outer layer will expand and engulf Mercury, Venus and even the Earth. This outer layer will eventually drift off into space, leaving just the exposed core, which will form a star type known as a white dwarf and then a black dwarf, which is essentially the remains of a dead star.

Questions To Answer:

1. What is the main fuel burnt in the Sun?

2. How long will the Sun keep burning for?

3. What type of star will it become once it has burnt up all its fuel?

Currently, the Sun is classified as a yellow dwarf star. As it uses up its fuel, it will turn into a red giant, then a white dwarf and finally a black dwarf. Draw this evolutionary sequence of the Sun, making sure that you draw each star type to the same scale.

Quick Fact: By the time the Sun turns into a red giant, and consumes the Earth, humans may well have developed the technology to be able to move to another planet, and possibly even one in another solar system. This means that even when the Sun dies, humanity may well be able to carry on.

Pop Quiz

The answers to all these questions can be found elsewhere in this book. See if you can answer them all!

1. What type of star is the Sun?
2. Which planet has the most moons?
3. How many planets are there in our solar system?
4. How big is our solar system?
5. What is the largest planet in our solar system?
6. What will happen when the Sun runs out of fuel?
7. How hot is the surface of the Sun?
8. Where is one of the coldest places in our solar system?
9. Where do most comets in our solar system come from?
10. What is an asteroid?
11. How fast does light from the Sun travel?
12. Can you name four places in our solar system, other than Earth, where some form of life might exist?
13. Which planet has the shortest day?
14. Why is Pluto no longer considered to be a planet?
15. What is the smallest planet in our solar system?
16. Which planet has the longest year?

From *Draw Your Own Encyclopaedia Our Solar System* by Colin M. Drysdale

Write Your Answers Here:

1. _____
2. _____
3. _____
4. _____
5. _____
6. _____
7. _____
8. _____
9. _____
10. _____
11. _____
12. _____
13. _____
14. _____
15. _____
16. _____

Pop Quiz – The Answers

1. Our sun is classified as a yellow dwarf star.
2. The planet with the most moons is Jupiter. At the last count, it had sixty-nine known moons.
3. There are eight planets in our solar system. These are Mercury, Venus, Earth, Mars, Jupiter, Saturn, Uranus and Neptune.
4. Our solar system is about 287 billion kilometres in diameter.
5. The largest planet in our solar system is Jupiter. It is 139,822 kilometres in diameter and weighs the same as 318 planet Earths.
6. When the Sun runs out of fuel, it will turn first into a red giant, then a white dwarf and, finally, a black dwarf.
7. The surface of the sun is 5,500 degrees centigrade.
8. One of the coldest places in our solar system is the south-western edge of Hermite Crater on the Moon. Here, temperatures can be as low as -247 °C!
9. Most comets come from the Oort Cloud, which lies at the very edge of our solar system.
10. Asteroids are pieces of rock that orbit the Sun, but that are too small to be considered planets. They are only found in the inner solar system, and most of them are found in the Asteroid Belt between Mars and Jupiter
11. The light from the Sun travels at 299,792 kilometres per second, and despite the 150 million kilometres that separate the Sun from the Earth, it only takes eight minutes for its light to reach us.
12. Potential candidates for places, other than Earth, where there may be life in our solar system include Mars, some of the moons of Jupiter and Saturn, and Pluto.
13. The planet with the shortest day is Jupiter. A day there lasts just under ten hours.
14. Pluto is no longer considered to be a planet because it has not managed to clear its orbit of other objects.
15. At 4,879 kilometres in diameter, the smallest planet in our solar system is Mercury.
16. The planet with the longest year is Neptune. A year there is almost 165 Earth years.

From *Draw Your Own Encyclopaedia Our Solar System* by Colin M. Drysdale

Where To Find Out More About Our Solar System

If you would like to brush up on your knowledge of our solar system, you can check out the following resources:

- **Wikipedia:** *en.wikipedia.org/wiki/Solar_System.*
- **Encyclopaedia Britannica:** *www.britannica.com/science/solar-system.*
- **The BBC:** *www.bbc.co.uk/science/space/solar system.*
- **The Wonders of the Solar System (TV Series):** Presented by Professor Brian Cox, this BBC television series is an excellent way to find out more about our solar system. It is available on DVD.
- **The Wonders of the Solar System (book):** This is an excellent book about the solar system written by Brian Cox and Andrew Cohen.

Online Content About Our Solar System That You Can Share With Your Class

Below is a list of free online videos about our solar system which are suitable for primary-age children and that you can share with your students:

- **An Introduction To Our Solar System:** Running time - 11 mins 54 secs. *https://youtu.be/Qd6nLM2QlWw.*
- **How Did Our Solar System Form:** Running time - 3 mins 53 secs. *https://youtu.be/IRZYMimUET8.*
- **What Is An Eclipse:** Running time - 4 mins 57 secs. *https://youtu.be/cxrLRbkOwKs.*
- **How To Get To Mars:** Running time - 6 mins 32 secs. *https://youtu.be/XRCIzZHpFtY.*
- **Welcome To Mars:** Running time - 4 mins 56 secs. *https://youtu.be/9I7HFpkYB9M.*
- **The Solar System Song:** Running time - 3 mins 8 secs. *https://youtu.be/mQrlgH97v94.*
- **How To Make A Model Solar System:** Running time - 9 mins 02 secs. *https://youtu.be/QkiQnkG-21k.*

Ideas For Additional Classroom Activities

These additional classroom activities can be used to add more interactive fun to learning about our solar system:

1. **Explore How Far Apart The Planets In Our Solar System Are:** To help your class understand the size of the solar system, take them outside into your school's playground, another open area or even a corridor in your school. Using chalk or any suitable marker, mark the location of the Sun at the centre of the solar system. Next, using 1 centimetre to represent 2 million kilometres, mark out the position of each planet (and Pluto). On this scale, Mercury will be 29 centimetres away from the Sun, Venus will be 54 centimetres away, Earth 75 cm away, Mars will be 114 cm away, Jupiter will be 389 cm away, Saturn will be 714 cm away, Uranus will be 1,436 cm away, Neptune will be 2,246 cm away and Pluto will be 2,913 cm away. The time it takes light from the Sun to reach each planet can be found on the additional information sheets at the end of this book.

2. **Create Scale Models Of The Planets In Our Solar System:** Divide your class into groups and get each group to make a model of an individual planet. Make sure that each group uses the same scale. These can then be used to create a model solar system to show how different in size the individual planets are. The easiest way to do this is to use different sizes of balloons to represent the planets. Information about the diameter of balloon needed for each planet using a scale of 1 cm to 2,000 km can be found on the additional information sheets at the end of this book. This activity can be combined with the one above which looks at the distances between all the planets in the solar system.

3. **Explore What Would Life Be Like On Other Planets:** Each planet is unique and life on each one would be very different. Look at how things like day length, year length, temperature, and body weight would vary between the different plants, and ask your class to imagine what it would be like living under these different conditions. You can find lots of useful information for this activity in the additional information sheets later in this book.

4. **Plan A Trip To Mars:** A typical trip to Mars would take between 150 and 250 days. Ask your students to plan a trip to Mars. Get them to decide on what size of spacecraft they'd need, where they'd get electricity from, how much oxygen they'd need to take to breathe for over 150 days, what medicines they would need to take, how they would exercise during the journey (to stop their muscles atrophying from lack of use), how they would keep themselves occupied, where they'd get food from, where they'd get water from, how they'd communicate with people back on Earth, how many people they'd want to take, whether they would want to take any pets, how much rocket fuel they'd need, how much toilet paper they'd need, and so on. Remember that if they wish to come back again, they would need to take enough supplies to do that too! You can also use this planning to think about how they could reduce the amount of stuff they'd need to take (such as using solar panels to generate electricity, recycling urine into drinking water, and growing plants using human waste as manure).

From *Draw Your Own Encyclopaedia Our Solar System* by Colin M. Drysdale

Handouts And Additional Information

On the following pages, you will find a variety of handouts and additional information that you can use during additional classroom activities to accompany the information provided in this book.

1. **Blank *Draw Your Own Encyclopaedia* Pages:** Ask you students to pick a planet or other object in our solar system and get them to create their own pair of *Draw Your Own Encyclopaedia* pages about it using these blank templates. Once they are finished, bring them all together to create your classes very own custom *Draw Your Own Encyclopaedia* all about our solar system.

2. **How Much Would A Bottle Of Milk Weigh On Different Planets?** This handout provides all the information your students need to work out how much a two-pint bottle of milk would weigh on different planets in our solar system. Once these weights have been calculated you can then take a series of two-pint milk bottles and fill them with just the right amount of air, water, sand and/or metal ball bearings so that the weight as much as they would on each planet. This provides a really nice practical demonstration of what these different weights would actually feel like.

3. **How Old Would You Be On Different Planets?** This handout provides all the information your students need to work out how old they would be on different planets in our solar system.

4. **Additional Information About How The Characteristics Of Different Planets Compare To Each Other:** This information can be used to create scale models of the planets using balloons, measure out the relative distances between the planets in your playground or compare day lengths and year lengths. It can also be used to play games of Higher-and-Lower, where you start with a particular characteristic of one planet, and your students have to guess whether this characteristic for the next planet you pick is greater or less than it is for the first one. This can be based on mass, diameter, day length, year length, or any other characteristic you wish to choose. A student handout version of this additional information table is also included which can be used to allow your students to calculate some of these values for themselves before making such comparisons.

From *Draw Your Own Encyclopaedia Our Solar System* by Colin M. Drysdale

Quick Fact:

Questions To Answer:

Quick Fact:

How Much Would A Bottle Of Milk Weigh On Other Planets?

Due to differences in size and the materials they are made from, the same object would weigh different amounts on each planet in our solar system. To work out how much an object would weigh on another planet, you first need to know its surface gravity relative to the Earth's. You can then multiply the object's weight on Earth by this number to get its weight on a different planet.

For example, a two-pint bottle of milk weighs 1,200 grams on Earth. The surface gravity on Mars is 0.38 of the surface gravity on Earth. When these two numbers are multiplied together (1,200 x 0.38), we get 456. So a two pint bottle of milk would only weigh 456 grams on Mars.

Here is a table of the relative surface gravity for each planet in our solar system (and Pluto). Use these values to work out how much a two-pint bottle of milk would weigh on each of these planets.

Planet	Relative Surface Gravity	Weight of two-pint bottle of milk
Mercury	0.38	
Venus	0.91	
Earth	1	
Mars	0.38	
Jupiter	2.36	
Saturn	0.92	
Uranus	0.89	
Neptune	1.12	
Pluto	0.06	

From *Draw Your Own Encyclopaedia Our Solar System* by Colin M. Drysdale

How Old Would You Be On Different Planets?

A year is defined as how long it takes a planet to complete a single orbit of the Sun. By comparing the length of time each planet takes to complete a single orbit to the length of a year on Earth, you can work out how old you would be on different planets, based on the length of a year there. You can do this by dividing your current age in Earth years by the relative year length of other planets.

For example, a year on Mars lasts 1.88 Earth years. So, if you are ten years old in Earth years, you would divide ten by 1.88 (10 ÷ 1.88) to get your age in Mars years. When you do this, you'd find that if you are ten years old on Earth, you would only be 5.32 years old on Mars!

Here is a table of the year length for each planet in our solar system (and Pluto) relative to an Earth year. Use these values to work out how old you would be on each of these planets.

Planet	Year Length Relative To A Earth Year	My Age On This Planet
Mercury	0.24	
Venus	0.61	
Earth	1	
Mars	1.88	
Jupiter	11.86	
Saturn	29.46	
Uranus	84.01	
Neptune	164.79	
Pluto	248.59	

Table Of Characteristics Of Different Objects In Our Solar System.

Created to provide additional classroom activities to accompany *Draw Your Own Encyclopaedia Our Solar System* by Colin M. Drysdale (ISBN: 978-10909832-46-6)

Astronomical Object	Size			Day length		Year Length		Distance to Sun	
	Diameter (km)	Scale 1cm = 2,000km	Size Ratio to Earth	Earth Days	Scale 1 sec = 24 hours	Earth Years	Scale 1 minute to one Earth Year	Million Km	Scale 1 cm = 2,000,000 km
Sun	1,391,016 km	695.5 cm	109.16	-	-	-	-	-	-
Mercury	4,880 km	2.44 cm	0.38	58.60	58.7 secs	0.24	14 secs	57.9	0.29 m
Venus	12,104 km	6.05 cm	0.95	243.00	243 secs	0.61	37 secs	108.2	0.54 m
Earth (Moon)	**12,742 km** (3,474 km)	**6.37 cm** (1.47 cm)	**1** (0.27)	**1.00** (28)	**1 sec** (28 sec)	**1**	**1 min**	**149.6**	**0.75 m**
Mars	6,780 km	3.39 cm	0.53	1.03	1 sec	1.88	1 min 53 secs	227.9	1.14 m
Jupiter	139,822 km	69.91 cm	10.97	0.42	0.43 secs	11.86	11 mins 52 secs	778.3	3.89 m
Saturn	116,464 km	58.23 cm	9.14	0.46	0.46 secs	29.46	29 mins 28 secs	1,427.0	7.14 m
Uranus	50,724 km	25.36 cm	3.98	0.71	0.71 secs	84.01	1 hour 24 mins 6 secs	2,871.0	14.36 m
Neptune	49,244 km	24.62 cm	3.86	0.67	0.67 secs	164.79	2 hours 44 mins 47 secs	4,491.1	22.46 m
Pluto (minor planet)	2,377 km	1.19 cm	0.19	6.38	6.38 secs	248.59	4 hours 8 mins 35 secs	5,913	29.13 m

Downloaded from PictishBeastPublications.com.

Astronomical Object	Mass (kg)	Mass ratio to Earth	How long does light from the Sun take to reach it?	How many moons does it have?	What is the average Surface temperature (min/max)?	How much would a 25 kg person weigh?	What is the mass ratio to weight on Earth?	How many local days in a local year?	How old would a ten year old be in local years?	How old would a ten year old be in local days?
Sun	1.989 x 10³⁰	333,000	-	-	5,550 °C (4,000 °C – 1,000,000+ °C)	697.5 kg	27.9	-	-	-
Mercury	0.330 x 10²⁴	0.055	3 mins 12 secs	0	167 °C (-184 °C to 465 °C)	9.5 kg	0.38	1.5	41	62
Venus	4.87 x 10²⁴	0.815	6 mins 0 secs	0	462 °C	22.75 kg	0.91	0.92	16	14
Earth (Moon)	**5.97 x 10²⁴** 0.073 x 10²⁴	**1** (0.01)	**8 mins 18 secs**	**1**	**14 °C** (-89.2 °C to 70.7 °C)	**25 kg** (4 kg)	**1** (0.16)	**365**	**10**	**3,653**
Mars	0.642 x 10²⁴	0.11	12 mins 36 secs	2	-55 °C (-153 °C to 20 °C)	9.5 kg	0.38	659.5	5	3,551
Jupiter	1898 x 10²⁴	318	43 mins 12 secs	69+	-145 °C	58.5 kg	2.34	10,394	0.84	8,814
Saturn	569 x 10²⁴	95	1 hour 19 mins 18 secs	62+	-178 °C	26.5 kg	1.06	23,448	0.34	8,327
Uranus	86.8 x 10²⁴	14.5	2 hours 59 mins 36 secs	27+	-224 °C	23 kg	0.92	51,655	0.12	5,071
Neptune	102 x 10²⁴	17	4 hours 6 mins	14+	-218 °C	29.75 kg	1.19	89,700	0.061	5,427
Pluto (minor planet)	0.0131 x 10²⁴	0.002	5 hours 30 mins	5	-223 °C	1.5 kg	0.06	14,233	0.040	570

Astronomical Object	Surface gravity (ms⁻²)	Surface gravity relative to Earth	If I can jump one metre on Earth, how high could I jump on other planets?	How much would a 2 pint bottle of milk weigh?	What is the escape velocity?	How long could I survive on its surface without a space suit?
Sun	273.42	27.9	0.036 m	33.48 kg	2,225,000 km/h	Instant vaporisation
Mercury	3.72	0.38	2.63 m	0.46 kg	15,300 km/h	Mercury always has the same side facing the Sun, so one side is really hot, and the other is really cold. If you landed at just the right point between these two sides, you would neither freeze to death, nor be boiled alive. Instead, since Mercury has no oxygen in its atmosphere, you'd survive as long as you could hold your breath (about two minutes)
Venus	8.92	0.91	1.10 m	1.09 kg	37,296 km/h	As the surface temperature is over 400 °C, you'd last less than one second before being boiled alive.
Earth (Moon)	**9.8** (1.62)	**1** (0.16)	**1 m** (6.25 m)	**1.2 kg** (0.192)	**40,269 km/h** (8,568 km/h)	**About 80 years.** (As long as you coul hold your breath.)
Mars	3.72	0.38	2.63 m	0.46 kg	18,1108 km/h	Although Mars is very cold, if you had warm enough clothes, you wouldn't instantly freeze to death. Instead, since there's no oxygen, you'd only be able to survive as long as you could hold your breath, so about two minutes.
Jupiter	23.13	2.36	0.42 m	28.32 kg	216,700 km/h	As Jupiter is a gas giant, it has no real surface. So, if you tried to land on it, you'd simply sink into it, where you'd be crushed to death by the massive pressures. This would happen in less than a second
Saturn	9.02	0.92	1.09 m	1.10 kg	129,900 km/h	As Saturn is a gas giant, it has no real surface. So, if you tried to land on it, you'd simply sink into it, where you'd be crushed to death by the massive pressures. This would happen in less than a second
Uranus	8.72	0.89	1.12 m	1.07 kg	76,938 km/h	As Uranus is a gas giant, it has no real surface. So, if you tried to land on it, you'd simply sink into it, where you'd be crushed to death by the massive pressures. This would happen in less than a second
Neptune	10.98	1.12	0.89 m	1.34 kg	84,816 km/h	As Neptune is a gas giant, it has no real surface. So, if you tried to land on it, you'd simply sink into it, where you'd be crushed to death by the massive pressures. This would happen in less than a second
Pluto (minor planet)	0.59	0.06	16.67 m	0.07 kg	4,428 km/h	With a surface temperature of -223 °C, and no breathable atmosphere, it would be a toss up as to whether you'd freeze to death before you ran out of oxygen and needed to take another breath. Either way, you'd be dead within a few minutes.

Table Of Characteristics Of Different Objects In Our Solar System.

Created to provide additional classroom activities to accompany *Draw Your Own Encyclopaedia Our Solar System* by Colin M. Drysdale (ISBN: 978-1090983246-6)

Astronomical Object	Size			Distance to Sun		Day Length		Year Length	
	Diameter (km)	Size Ratio to Earth	Scale 1cm = 2,000km	Million Km	Scale 1 cm = 2,000,000 km	Earth Days	Scale 1 sec = 24 hours	Earth Years	Scale 1 minute to one Earth Year
Sun	1,391,016 km	109.16		-	-	-	-	-	-
Mercury	4,880 km	0.38		57.9		58.60		0.24	
Venus	12,104 km	0.95		108.2		243.00		0.61	
Earth (Moon)	**12,742 km** (3,474 km)	**1** (0.27)		**149.6**		**1.00** (28)		**1**	
Mars	6,780 km	0.53		227.9		1.03		1.88	
Jupiter	139,822 km	10.97		778.3		0.42		11.86	
Saturn	116,464 km	9.14		1,427.0		0.46		29.46	
Uranus	50,724 km	3.98		2,871.0		0.71		84.01	
Neptune	49,244 km	3.86		4,491.1		0.67		164.79	
Pluto (minor planet)	2,377 km	0.19		5,913		6.38		248.59	

Downloaded from *PictishBeastPublications.com*.

Astronomical Object	How long does light from the Sun take to reach it?	Mass (kg)	Mass ratio to Earth mass	If the Earth weighed 1kg, how much would each planet weigh?	Surface gravity relative to Earth	How much would a 2 pint bottle of milk weigh on each planet?	If you can jump one metre on Earth, how high could you jump on other planets?	How many local days in a local year?	How old would a ten year old be in local years?	How old would a ten year old be in local days?
Sun	-	1.989 x 10^{30}	333,000		27.9					
Mercury	3 mins 12 secs	0.330 x 10^{24}	0.055		0.38					
Venus	6 mins 0 secs	4.87 x 10^{24}	0.815		0.91					
Earth (Moon)	**8 mins 18 secs**	**5.97 x 10^{24}** 0.073 x 10^{24}	**1** (0.01)	**1 kg** (0.01 kg)	**1** (0.16)	**1.200 kg** (0.192 kg)	**1m** (6.25m)	365	10	3650
Mars	12 mins 36 secs	0.642 x 10^{24}	0.11		0.38					
Jupiter	43 mins 12 secs	1898 x 10^{24}	318		2.36					
Saturn	1 hour 19 mins 18	569 x 10^{24}	95		0.92					
Uranus	2 hours 59 mins	86.8 x 10^{24}	14.5		0.89					
Neptune	4 hours 6 mins	102 x 10^{24}	17		1.12					
Pluto (minor planet)	5 hours 30 mins	0.013 x 10^{24}	0.002		0.06					

Books available now in the *Draw Your Own Encyclopaedia* series from Pictish Beast Publications:

1. **Mammals** - ISBN: 978-1-909832-39-8. RRP: UK: £6.99 US: $8.99.
2. **Birds** - ISBN: 978-1-909832-41-1. RRP: UK: £6.99 US: $8.99.
3. **Reptiles** - ISBN: 978-1-909832-42-8. RRP: UK: £6.99 US: $8.99.
4. **Amphibians** - ISBN: 978-1-909832-43-5. RRP: UK: £6.99 US: $8.99.
5. **Fish** - ISBN: 978-1-909832-44-2. RRP: UK: £6.99 US: $8.99.
6. **Invertebrates** - ISBN: 978-1-909832-45-9. RRP: UK: £6.99 US: $8.99.
7. **Animals Box Set** – ISBN: 978-1-909832-51-0. RRP: UK: £39.99 US:$49.99.
8. **Scotland's Dolphins** - ISBN: 978-1-909832-55-8. RRP: UK: £6.99 US: $8.99.
9. **Scotland's Seabirds** - ISBN: 978-1-909832-59-6. RRP: UK: £6.99 US: $8.99.
10. **Scotland's Native Wildlife** - ISBN: 978-1-909832-62-6. RRP: UK: £6.99 US: $8.99.
11. **Scotland's Castles** - ISBN: 978-1-909832-61-9. RRP: UK: £6.99 US: $8.99.
12. **Scotland's Folklore** - ISBN: 978-1-909832-63-3. RRP: UK: £6.99 US: $8.99.
13. **Our Solar System** - ISBN: 978-1-909832-46-6. RRP: UK: £6.99 US: $8.99
14. **Hebridean Marine Life** – ISBN: 978-1-909832-54-1. RRP: UK: £6.99 US: $8.99

Books coming soon in the *Draw Your Own Encyclopaedia* series:

1. **Planet Earth** - ISBN: 978-1-909832-50-3 RRP: UK: £6.99 US: $8.99.
2. **Deep Space** - ISBN: 978-1-909832-47-3. RRP: UK: £6.99 US: $8.99.
3. **The Universe** - ISBN: 978-1-909832-48-0. RRP: UK: £6.99 US: $8.99.
4. **Space Exploration** - ISBN: 978-1-909832-49-7. RRP: UK: £6.99 US: $8.99.

For more information on this series of books (including a full list of available and upcoming titles), visit: *www.pictishbeastpublications.com/draw-your-own-encyclopaedia*

www.ingramcontent.com/pod-product-compliance
Lightning Source LLC
Chambersburg PA
CBHW050716090526
44587CB00019B/3403